BOOK 3

Especially in *Romantic Style*

7 Lyrical Solos for Late Intermediate Pianists

Dennis Alexander

Music written in romantic style is instantly appealing and some of the most accessible in terms of interpretation. Much of the music from the Romantic era was written especially for the piano. *Especially in Romantic Style* was written for pianists who love the expressive qualities of this instrument and the sounds of the romantic style. The warm, lyrical melodies and the rich harmonies of these pieces will appeal to pianists of any age. Through this music, students can learn to play with a beautiful tone, listen to each note, and shape musical phrases, preparing them to study the great Romantic period piano masterpieces of Chopin, Mendelssohn and Schumann. It is my hope that each of these musical vignettes will inspire students to create a beautiful sound and to play with expressiveness, musicality and finesse.

With all best wishes,

Dennis Alexander

This collection is dedicated with great pride and joy to my colleague and former student, Amy Grinsteiner.

ISBN-10: 0-7390-6093-7
ISBN-13: 978-0-7390-6093-3

Alfred

Serenity

Dennis Alexander

A Special Someone

Dennis Alexander

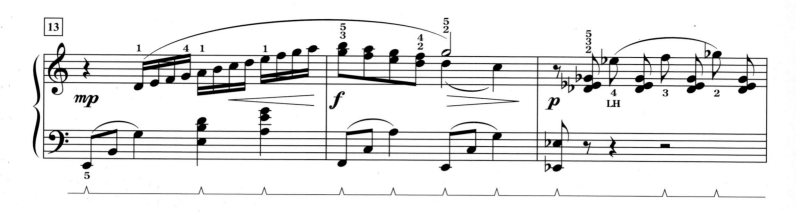

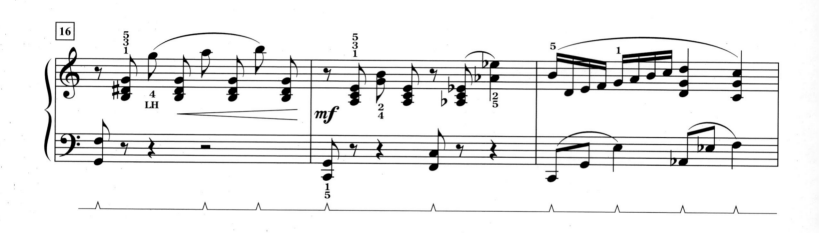

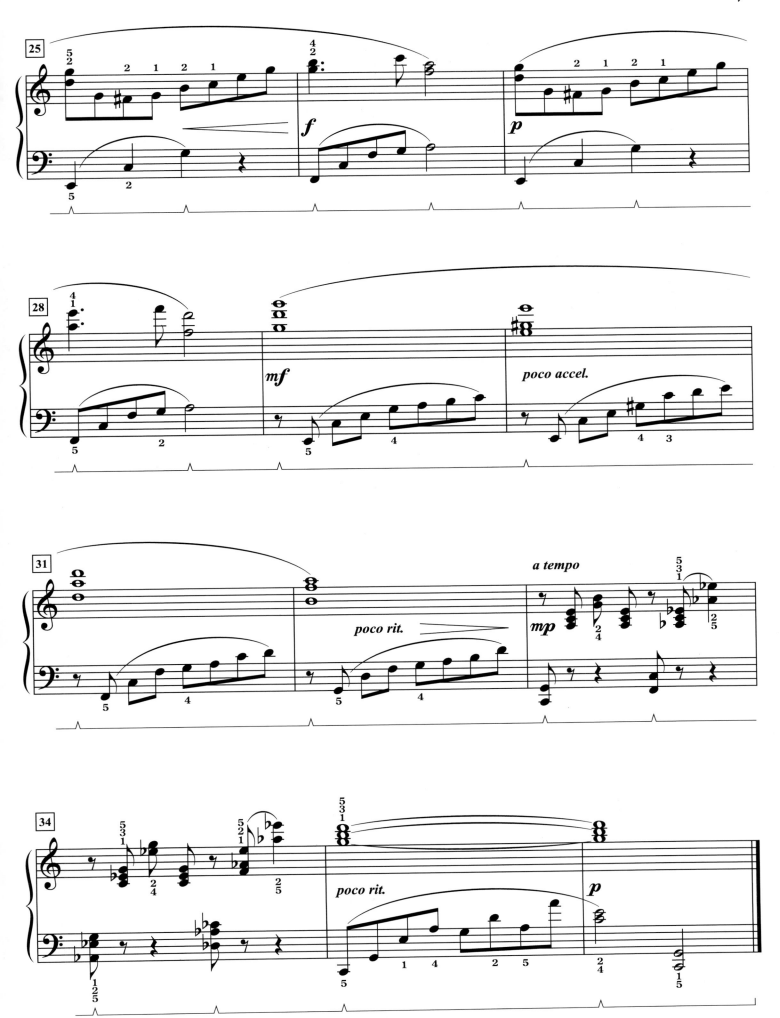

Midnight Meditation

Dennis Alexander

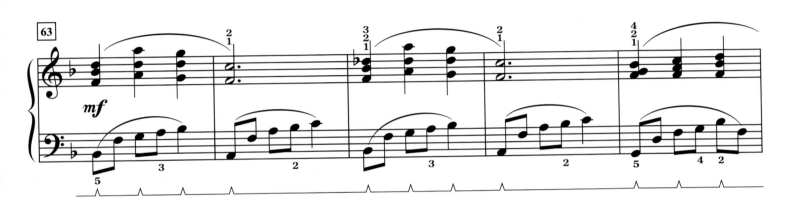

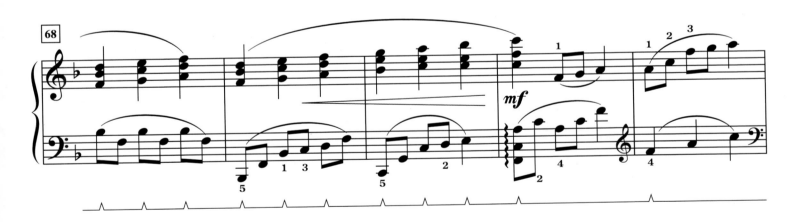

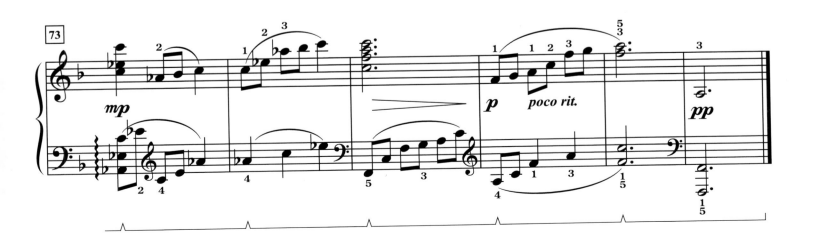

In a Dancin' Mood

Dennis Alexander

Improvisation No. 1

Dennis Alexander

The Promise of Spring

Dennis Alexander

Evocation

Dennis Alexander

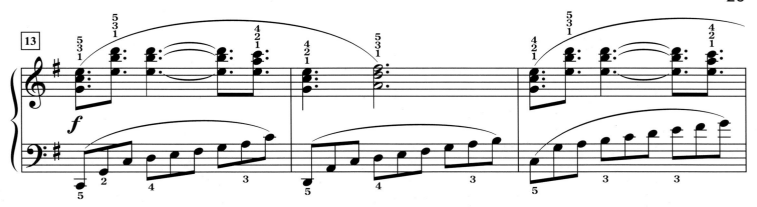

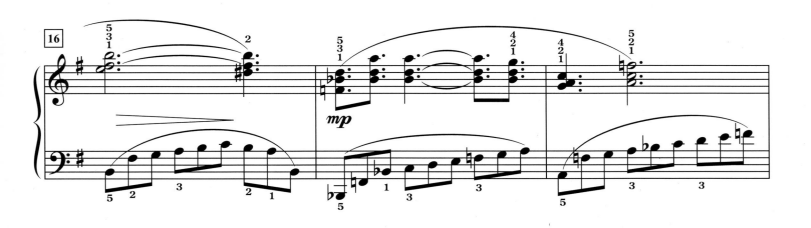

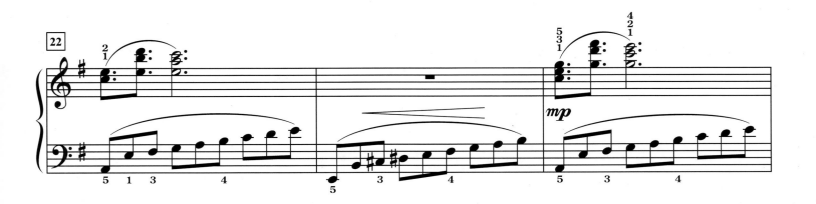